EXPLODING HEAD

EXPLODING HEAD

POEMS
CYNTHIA MARIE HOFFMAN

PERSEA BOOKS
A Karen & Michael Braziller Book

Persea Books, Inc.
90 Broad Street
New York, New York 10004

LIBRARY OF CONGRESS CATALOGING-IN-PUBLICATION DATA

Names: Hoffman, Cynthia Marie, author.
Title: Exploding head : poems / Cynthia Marie Hoffman.
Description: New York, New York : Persea Books, A Karen & Michael Braziller Book, 2024.
    | Summary: "Prose poems chronicling a woman's childhood onset of, and adult journey
    through, obsessive-compulsive disorder (OCD)"—Provided by publisher.
Identifiers: LCCN 2023038906 (print) | LCCN 2023038907 (ebook) |
    ISBN 9780892555772 (paperback ; acid-free paper) | ISBN 9780892555819 (e-book)
Subjects: LCSH: Mentally ill women—Poetry. | Obsessive-compulsive disorder—Poetry. |
    LCGFT: Prose poems.
Classification: LCC PS3608.O47765 E97 2024 (print) | LCC PS3608.O47765 (ebook) |
    DDC 811/.6—dc23/eng/20231002
LC record available at https://lccn.loc.gov/2023038906
LC ebook record available at https://lccn.loc.gov/2023038907

Book design and composition by Rita Lascaro
Typeset in Arno Pro
Manufactured in the United States of America. Printed on acid-free paper.

CONTENTS

1.

2.

3.

4.

EXPLODING HEAD

1.

Smoke When You Can't See What's on Fire

Somewhere off the road, a fire burns, and you are not you again today. In the distant sky, a bird has gotten hold of a fat snake of smoke and is wrangling it out from the treetops, while down below, a woman lies in the burning house where the bright hot tongue of the snake is lashing. Secretly, slipped behind a bed skirt, a child's collection of feathers melts inside its miniature cardboard room. You drive the road home, and the wind rips scales from the snake's body, bits of ash flickering against the sky. It's sort of beautiful. The whole hillside catches fire in the sunlight. The bird lets go. You are not you again today, having tied the smoke around your throat like a scarf. You wear it at night as you sleep. In the forest, the child runs barefoot, torn dress flapping behind her. A light flickers in the leaves. She will build a new house, beginning with her one brick of feathers. You have a child, too, asleep in the other room, dreaming her rough-pelted teddy has come alive. In the morning, she says she saw his bones in the x-ray machine and his beating heart. But inside his bones were tiny germs. There is a gift you want to leave her with. And it is not this worry. *It's okay*, she says. *Baby Bear just needs his medicine. It's okay*.

Like This

The bad part of your mind was still asleep when you walked with your mother at the playground's edge. *Like this*, you said, and she lifted the camera. Crouched among ferns, you almost couldn't feel the soft arrows pointing you out from all directions. Meanwhile, your sister's swing swished and lulled, the blur of her yellow dress. The bad part of your mind was a leaf slick in the rain, a slug clinging to the leaf. Not even your mother knew it was there. In the picture, ringlets dangle at your ears. Even then, whispers funneled through their halls. The smear of light that trailed behind your sister's body dissolved and was drawn again. What did you think your life would become? Tonight, the moon with barely a face formed on it.

The Angel

The angel stands in your room, its presence a dense swelling in the dark. You lie in bed. You are afraid of angels. You sleep. You wake. The angel wants its whisper swirling in your ear. If it gets the chance, the angel leans over the bed. You wake. You sleep. Your pale ear glows in the dark, a whorl of petals parading the tunnel to your child brain. Cover your ear. You have been chosen. The angel is going to tell you the secret of heaven. Bury your ear in the quilt. The angel never leaves you. You sleep. You wake. One ear in the pillow, one ear in the quilt. The angel breathes. What else can you do? The quilt is a field of tiny pink flowers.

The Music of Language Is Clamping Down Hard

Your sister has spotted the woodpecker through the kitchen window. Every thought has a rhythm. The window, like all windows, has six lines: the lines around the outside and the X you draw in your mind, corner to corner. The forest is a thick enchantment of green. You're in your bare feet. Everyone leans toward the glass. You are just a girl in the summertime drawing the window in your mind: one two three four five six. Then the red flash of bird. *Isn't he humongous*, your mother says. Big as a cat. *Isn't he humongous* works on the window. Put the words on the window. The woodpecker clutches the feeder swinging by a rope. One two three four five six. Think again, *Isn't he humongous*. At your shoulder, your sister is normal, simple. But the music of language is opening up for you. The music of language is clamping down hard. When the woodpecker is gone, two slender birds sit together on a branch facing opposite directions, marking an X with their tails in the wide green glass.

It Starts

It starts when you are alone in your room, looking up at the window with pink curtains. You count the edges of the window. Right left top bottom. Vaguely you understand not to look at the corners where the edges touch. Beyond the window, minnows swarm the creek, each a slim number 1, tallying each other as they pass. Tick, tick, tick, tick in the dark beneath the eroded tree. The curtains are covered with constellations of glow-in-the-dark stars because you are not allowed to stick them on the ceiling. The curtains hide the corners of the window, but you know they are there, just as you know the minnows are there in the cool water. Everything is all right. The pattern of your counting makes a 4. When the light goes out, the stars illuminate two paths converging toward the heavens.

The Face Has Seven Holes

Someone is talking to you. Look at her face when she's talking to you. Draw a star. Start with the right nostril. Draw a line to the left ear, up to the right eye, down to the mouth, left eye, right ear, left nostril. The face has seven holes. Blink on it. Seven blinks. Her deep black eyes. One two three four moving mouth. Five six seven. In gym class, a volleyball hits you in the face. Your eye swells. *Is that why you're blinking so much*, someone says. She leans her face in. Seven fourteen twenty-one twenty-eight. This behavior is evident. You look like an idiot. Thirty-five forty-two forty-nine. Her moving lips. Fifty-six sixty-three. Her face has seven holes. Seventy. Did she say something? Draw a star. Blink on it.

You Get a Thought in Your Head

You sit on the stoop, staring at your hand. A prickly fat hedgehog waddles along the fence. The space between your thumb and your middle finger is a zero, and the sound is swish. But the sharp snap in your sister's palm is a twig breaking. Why can't you make that sound? You get a thought in your head. Your sister runs in the dappled yard in her shorts, cracking shafts of sunlight open with her thumbs. The concrete stings your legs. You get a thought in your head, and it's carving a hollow in your chest. In the afternoon, your mother takes you across the street to the neighbor's yard where you pick a raspberry from the trellis. The quiet hall of leaves. In your palm, a pinkish bulbous heart. A deeply scooped-out emptiness. Sweet sweet fruit. The only one who ever told you you were stupid was you.

Recording Angel

A tower of eyes, tall as a man. Wings fashioned from the feathery hairs of our human ears that sway with the smallest murmur. If the angel hears your dreams, he doesn't brush even the worst of them away. He lets them chew like moths on the ruffles of your brain. In the dollhouse, a teddy bear tall as a thumb turns its head on a pin. You have read the miniature Holy Bible with the magnifying glass the neighbor boys used to raise smoke from the backs of ants. The angel has no eyelids, nothing to blink with. Under the blanket, arms pressed between your legs, you grip tightly to your feet. So you can't be unfolded and led into the fire as you sleep.

You Believe

After a while, the stuffed animals begin to write letters. But you can never catch them doing it. Each afternoon, the turning of your small hand on the doorknob freezes their magic. Notepapers float to the carpet. *Dear Cindy*. Square boats on the square waters of your childhood. You put an ear against their fur but hear only the deep tangle of stuffing, perhaps a heart vanishing into the fog inside their chests. You had ridden the bus from school, pricked your shoulder on the bushes at the driveway. Sat on the floor, picking a blade of grass from your shin. These small disappointments. In the evenings, you gather the animals onto your bed, their weight negligible in your arms. Beyond the window, an airplane pens a long white line. Even as you sleep, you believe. The silver creek lights its crooked way through the forest, bending from somewhere to somewhere else. The animals clutch against the slim gate of innocence that has not yet closed in your heart.

Scar

You walk neatly in line through the halls, torrent of curls plaited to a drizzle down your back. Learn to spell *precipitation* and recite the letters in melody in front of class. When your hand slits open on the metal edge of a bulletin board, you tell no one, embarrassed by your ordinary humanness dripping onto the library carpet. Your body is made of light and spirit. You aren't supposed to bleed. At night, you run from the shadows seeping through the keyhole. Lie in bed counting and recounting the four boundaries of the world that open and close for you—windows, walls, pages, doorways. The floor-length mirror is a waterfall silvery with moonlight, thundering with the threat of drowning. One two three four. It was exhausting being good. Even now, all these years later, you are still tired. Your hand still bears the scar, a thin white wave cresting.

In the Forest

Deep in the forest behind the house, you are brilliantly alone. You overturn a stone. A salamander skitters on its belly. The forest is a bucket of trees, and you never think about your mother's eyes in the window on the hill. Your shadow ripples in the creek. You are a haunted girl, haunted of mind. A storm brews on the reflected world thick with Jesus bugs darting across the surface. One two three four black stick bodies. Five six insects hauling crosses on their backs. The cross that jabs seven times from somewhere deep inside your head, deeper than the eyes from the window can ever see. Once, you saw an eel suspended in the water. Once, you came upon a body made of crumbling bones and fur. A tunnel of light shimmering with dust was the animal's soul ascending through the canopy. You never wondered if it wasn't. Seven fourteen twenty-one twenty-eight. Because down in the trees, it is just you and God. And there is only one God.

Angel Number Seven

The seven angels gave you the multiplication table of sevens to recite like a prayer. As soon as you could count, seven clouds appeared in the water trough. Seven guinea hens are taken by the coyote. Goats faint. Deepwater fish slow their heart rates until they are undetectable. Horses spook and run into the fence, tearing open a shoulder to reveal an omen of seven cracks in the scapula. This paddle-shaped bone rows you home at dusk when the stars are tossed to the throwing cloth. It wards off the future, until the future comes. The skull of the mouse inches through the owl's intestines, turning its head in denial.

Conkers

Once, you smuggled home some of the blue stones that marked the graves beyond the hedge. For the time you secretly held them, pressing indentations in your palm, they seemed like hardened lumps of water, the possibility of transformation. You might become something else, like the dead. The kids swing horse chestnut seeds, bigger than marbles, from a string. The object is to bash open the wrinkled meat inside. But when they swing and miss, they seem to be knocking at an invisible door that hangs between them, and that is worse. You have your own game, and you must play it quietly in your mind, just as the dead must swim in the field alone, each in their own rectangular pool. The rules are: count the sides of the rectangles. Graves. Gravestones. The rules are: if you don't count, you'll die. When the seeds of the maple tree whirl to the street, you peel the wing apart to find a moist green brain with the idea of a tree enclosed in its folds. Maybe the seed in your brain will never become anything. But there is magic in the game that barricades the door from opening.

This Is All True

If your foot dangles off the edge of the bed, a metal blade rises from the floor and slices it off. The blade has already been installed in the floor. How do you know you haven't murdered someone accidentally? Look directly at the sun. Touch your eyeball once a day. Bite a hole in your cheek. Run to bed and lie perfectly still beneath the quilt before the toilet stops flushing. Something will happen if you don't. Press your fingers to your palm in a particular order. Don't blink while looking at something upsetting, like knives or illness or graves. Blinking seven times memorizes the faces of the people you love. This knock on the door is the police coming to take you away. Everything can be taken away in a blink. This could be your last day of freedom.

Touched

Lately, you get a feeling you might die. The world squeezes in on itself. A cloud is a hundred elephants, and the northern pike surface from the marsh like blimps. All day, you drive into this gradually compacting atmosphere. You worry what will happen to your body without you, how they will haul it away with all its secrets. You know what goes on. Many times, you've dissected what didn't belong to you, plucking the cattail's tightly packed muscle, fiber by fiber, exposing its cottony threads to the wind. What right do you have not to be touched? At night, you tighten the sheet so you can't be unwrapped from its camouflage of flowers and leaves. If the descending ceiling is still there tomorrow, snapping the necks of trees with its leaden hand, how will you go on? Soon there will be no difference between underground and aboveground. Birds bomb through the air like the skulls of galloping horses. Eventually, you will be laid down on a cold tray in a cold room where your body will be opened and made to weep into a drain, whirlpooling like the reddening smear of light across the event horizon just before the black hole, the most devastating sunset of your life, beyond which nothing can return. Not even these hands that held the tender naked core of the cattail heart. When winter comes, one goose sits on the ice. Another slips into the water.

Diagnosis

How would you characterize the counting? Drawing a star on the face of everyone you meet. Right now, are you counting these windows? Yes, but only the edges that make the windows. What is the thing you are most afraid of? Dying. The star peels from your face and floats through the window. In the mornings, you descend the stairs counting the railings of the banister. They rise as hammers inside a piano to make a silent music in your palm. Beyond the window, star-shaped leaves dangle in the tree, turning on their thin necks. What are you afraid of? Dying. The wind in their faces.

2.

Exploding Head Syndrome

You are finally an adult living with roommates in a house with a rickety banister and soft spots in the floor when your head begins exploding at night. First, a swish like a heavy wing dragging across the air, and then the door slams. Where does one life end and another begin? When you were a child, your thumb or your mother's thumb was slammed in the car door. One of you felt the pain, one of you the guilt. But you cannot remember which was which. You often dreamed of a guilt so grave you fell to your knees in the garden. Tadpoles shuddered in their leafy beds. What have you done? Once, a red balloon sailed to the ceiling of a warehouse, and though the ribbon slipped from your or your sister's fingers, you cannot remember which, you know the empty hand. You are always running from the shadow that chases you. In the forest at night, an owl screams a womanly, murderous scream. Neighbors call the police. You and your sister and your mother set out with the dog and a flashlight and find nothing.

You with the Getting Shot

It is a crisp autumn day when you get shot walking by the parking lot on your way to the lake. An arm goes up. A gun blows a hard kiss. You continue down the path, stepping around the acorns. You already got shot twice this morning. Always, you with the getting shot. You need to just let it pass. The lake goes on dragging the heavens this way and that. Your skin grows over the bullet. You sit at the shore with your back to the park pavilion where someone dismounts a bicycle and pulls out a gun. Your body fills like a penny jar with bullets. Heavy on the park bench. You watch the clouds getting snarled in rippling water, angels drowning in their tangled skirts. Someone creeps in the trees. Someone's breathing down your back. There are no bones left in your body that aren't a clattering procession of bullets. You just need to rest for a bit by the lake. One after another, the white knots bob toward the shore but never fully arrive. Even if they did, even if they tumbled gasping at your feet in their gauzy threads, you with your buckshot hands, your mind a shuddering animal hunkered down inside your skull, heaven help you, couldn't do a thing about it.

Simultaneity

The smallest thing sets off a spark. A cigarette careening down the highway like a tiny seagull with its tail on fire. Fire in the belly of the car. Today marks the opening of the southern portal in the sky. Geese are honking their way out of here. It is the first cool evening of the year when the car explodes. Your lap spangles with glass. Meanwhile, the lake has swallowed a cloud. The lake is slick as a skull, and you go charging deep into its watery brain. Meanwhile, your hands are on the wheel. You drive until the garage door lifts an eyelid, awakening the bright eye of home. By now, the hair of the drowned woman has wiped away her face. You carry her with you, dripping across the kitchen tiles. The water is already boiling on the stove. Your husband hands you the knife. Meanwhile, the first geese of autumn fly through the blue door.

Quality of Life

Part of the problem is that you were in a horrific accident on your way here, and you are already dead. Your body disrobes. The skins of your hands float freely in the marsh, starfish among the cattails. But would you say your quality of life is affected? You've left a dozen bodies behind just today. One drowned in the bathtub. Several wandering blindly in the kitchen, clanging into each other like windchimes. One floats inside the sunken car just below the overpass. Now that it's getting dark, the frogs are springing from their cool, fat bellies. Who will come in wading boots to scoop your palms into a net? You are just vapor and light, pooled loosely in this chair, neither ghost nor angel. Right at this moment, an airplane is crashing through the roof.

Ruminate

As a cow turned out to pasture ruminates, your mind, reclined to feathers at night, chews on the thought of death. Memento mori. The mind is a muscular tongue that never tires. Years ago, you learned even the docile cow is capable of violence. Alone in a field far from the road lined with hedges, you could have been trampled to death but weren't. The beast stopped in time. It showed its eye was a quarry of night and gave you all the darkness you could carry. When you finally arrived, the stones that had fallen from the crumbling church were nowhere to be found in the tall grass but had instead lifted away like seeds. What if you cast your thoughts like that to the wind? But instead, each night, the tongue returns to work the unchewable bone.

Blood Moon

The night of the lunar eclipse, you step between the red curtain and the window, toddler on your hip. The way you'd promised her the moon, the child expected a bloody, murderous scene splashed across the night and is unimpressed in her half-dreams by this single droplet suspended in the sky. This blister already reabsorbing its own blood. You wear the blood red curtain like a cloak of blood, a long blood mane, exposed as the wild and frightened animal you are. Nothing stays whole forever. But this child, swaddled in blankets, is without a scratch tonight and easily returned to her dreams. The bloodshot eye has closed, and you should sleep now, too. The world isn't as scary as you'd have her believe. And now she knows it.

Intersection

In your mind, a garden a street runs through. In the bedroom, a nightlight. The street crosses another street. Intersection of a child struck with light. Of headlights and nightlights. The night is a wall and so is the wall. Intersection of road and four black planets rolling. Intersection of ladybug rain boots. Of running. Of the small hand that rips from the hand that is heavy. Intersection of running. Light on the wall is light on the body struck with light. Of the child's nightgown beyond the wall inflating, deflating. Your head on the pillow wherein the impact. Of the hammering of light. Of the nail loose in your heart. On one side of the wall, fear, and on the other, the small immaculate accordion singing sweet sleep in the night.

House Inside the House

One night, the wing drags across your face. You rise and go with the angel through the closet door. He shows you the house inside the house. A secret circular window that opens to an ocean. A room of ornate wooden chairs. A giant moth gliding down the hall in an evening gown. In this room, all the black spots on your humid heart are bristling into a furry mold. For the first time, you can see the angel's face, slick as an oyster shell. How could he possess such luminance, having no mouth to swallow the light with? In the kitchen, a tower of sugar cubes stacked to the ceiling. It burns your teeth.

None of This Happened

Babies in pots on the windowsill you forgot to water. Men pushing on the door while you push back from the other side. They have knives. They have big hands. They cling to the hood of the car as you drive. A wall of lockers with bodies spilling out. Your job is to stuff the arms and legs back in and shut the doors. The red and slippery floor. The squeak of your shoe. The emergency line will call you back. The back of your head is blown open. The nurse doesn't care. The phone is dead. No one wants to hear about your dreams. Baby in a milk jug you left in the fridge where it is dark and cold. Hauling trash bags of babies uphill. Someone you know is still alive with broken legs. You try to carry him, but beyond the doors, the world is on fire. Opening the doors to a wing of the house you never knew was there but has been here all along. Standing on rocks by the river as the sun sets. More beauty than you have ever seen in real life. Going down the water slide in the rain. You miss the bus. You take the wrong train. Years later, the stickiness of your own blood is still on your hand.

Float

Why is your face so red? You need to relax. You should take your body off. Lift your skull off your body and hook it on the hat rack by the door. Float into the back yard filled with light. Let's end this now. You're the favorite. You have so much to be happy about. None of it is your fault. But you're sorry. You've disappointed everyone, and you're sorry.

Balaclava

It is cold where you live. The streets darken early. People stand at the bus stop in ski masks and shoot at you with their guns. Your face is a bullseye glowing in the windshield. There is no way home except to drive this thin lane through the trees. Just beyond the headlight's boundary, a glint of eyes, ghost of breath. Puff of air displaced by the bullet leaving the chamber. Remember, you are no longer a child and should not be afraid of a masked stranger on the street. In the house by the garden shriveled with frost, your husband waits. The fire burns in its cage. Look for his smoke signal. The stars stare down your every move from the anonymity of their balaclavas. Steady your hand on the wheel. You will know when the bullet is about to hit because the windshield shatters first.

Corpse Meditation

Your bedroom is a tomb. Outside the window, a hawk on a streetlight lifts the night's curtain in its talons to unveil the second act of light. There is a religious practice that imagines the moments after death. But that's not what this is. Mothers worry what would become of their children. But that's not what this is. It begins to snow. You imagine your daughter comes into the room, just tall enough to peer over the mattress, her forehead damp with dreams. You are not asleep but cannot be roused. What happens next? Do you watch her from above? Reach to her with your non-hands? You cling so tightly to this world. It is the reason your mind obsesses over leaving it. The more you meditate on death, the more you are protected from it. The hawk in the night is a talisman. Crystals of light collapse against the house. Your child's tiny winter boots by the back door wait for morning.

Field Guide to the Proper Identification
of Roadside Debris

Shoe with the ghost of a foot pressed inside. Straw with a tooth wedged. The raccoon's stare. A pacifier. Fog. Garbage bags jutting with elbows. A leaf hightailing it across in the breeze. Battered suitcases zippered shut with kidnapped children. The blinding sun. Thump under the wheel. The sound you carry home with you at night, like a bird dropping its prey on the roof. The key to identification lies in the unseen. The shattered bone. It doesn't mean you're not a gentle person. The leaf that is a bullfrog. The snake that is a hoodie string. Flattened gumballs dotting the way to your destination. Red, yellow, green. This bridge you must cross. And a snarl of rags rolling down the road, nothing at its heart but wind.

Open Window

Children are sucked into the night. A gasp opens in the wall. You wake and drag the curtains from the wind. Your child sleeps, but it doesn't matter. Enormous moths sail in and smother children in their sleep. In darkness, her cheek's pale wing. An airplane falls out of the night. She wears a yellow nightie. The cheetah wears a yellow nightie and stares with unlidded eyes. Children sleepwalk onto the roof. You straighten her curtains like slim guards standing at attention. And beyond the window, the street glimmers like a black river heaving a galaxy of stars. The nightlight's stars dispatch from the ceiling and float through the room. Stars sizzle on the warmth of her arms like golden snowflakes. Close your robe against your own rampant heart. You are trying to let them burn.

Intrusive

The heron stabs through the meniscus because it is stalking and ravenous, but you are gentle, even with this knife in your hand. It is natural to wonder if you might kill someone. This thought is not an intruder who shatters the bedroom window but the fish that hatches already in the water. The human mind is intrinsically capable of fearsome things. Peer through any window, and you will find the same gray snarl of fish. But this too shall pass. As the fish swims, the water splits to receive it, tumbles from glossy eye to ragged tail and rejoins, unharmed. You are innocent of all the violent things your thoughts imagine doing. Don't be upset. Your mind can be the water the fish slides right through.

Stipulations

One day you will find a body in a grassy ditch near the road, just as you imagined. The trash bag flaps in the wind. But the body won't belong to anyone, and no one is dead. These are your stipulations. One day you will be shot in the arm. You will stay in the hospital long enough for yellow tulips wheeled in on a cart. A man will come into the house to attack your family, but no one will be scared. You will wrestle for the gun and shoot him in the head, but it won't make a mess on the crisp white walls. And he won't actually be dead. These are your stipulations. You will be in a head-on collision on a bendy road flanked by trees. A figure in a heavy coat will use the jaws of life. He will smell of smoke. And when you lie in bed, the angel who's been waiting in the shadows your entire life approaches and whispers the secret of heaven. He is full of light. You are wide awake. And you will live forever.

3.

Seven Darknesses

No one knows how dark the darkness is. A bat flaps from the hay barn dressed in a shawl of webs. Call to the night. It answers with a thud against the neighbor's house. It screams like a fox at the gate. The black spots on your heart grow blacker. You might never cast off your darknesses. One trots beside you like a black hole on a leash, barking. No one was meant to live at absolute zero, absolute dark. The earth itself cannot imagine it. Its oceans are strung with lanternfish like fairy lights. Tonight, this spongy cloud blotting copies of the moon across the sky. The warmth of your body emits a single photon detectable by the most sensitive machinery. And then another. And then this fog slipping into your pocket like a ghostly hand, seeking comfort.

The Phantom

One night, when you were still a child, the phantom lunged for your neck. Come morning, it was still hanging on, so you wore its darkness behind you, fluttering down the stairs like a cape. What else could you have done? It grew as you grew into adulthood, ravenous, hoarding your secrets. When you walk in the street, its threads tangle with cans and bottle caps rattling behind you as from a wedding car. You're afraid you will be together forever, across all the seasons. When you lie in bed with your husband, the third body lies with you. In the snow, it sweeps away the evidence of your steps. On rainy days, it's heavy as a crash test dummy pulled from a watery plane wreck. Look at you, taking on the hunch of an old woman, bearing its weight. Eventually, it will push you to the deepest trenches. When will you stop this? Even now, your beloved has climbed the ladder and begun to hang lights in the tree. See how, from down here, they illuminate the underbellies of the leaves so they look like the hulls of boats, each one a chance to resurface?

Uncle's Gun

No one said it would hurt as much as it did. The dogs raced around, grunting, anticipating a bird to drop. *Don't be so sensitive,* your sister always said. You aimed for a feathery, untouchable cloud and pulled the trigger. The force had already blasted across the valley before you could take it back. Animals crouched in their burrows. Deep in the lavender field, a bumble bee retracted its tongue from a flower. Even the gun recoiled. That night, your shoulder ached. You slept on the hard floor, forever marked. You will never not be a person who fired a gun. That single shot reverberating in the dirt beneath the foundation where you lay down your head.

Dark Matter

Anything not cold is not fear. This is the rule of night. Blanket pulled tight against your lips, warm kiss of armor. There are various densities of dark, a shadow inside a shadow. You never see the knife, but you know it's there. Nor the man, but you wait for him. The forest leans over the house. You dare not move, but your mind moves, hardening shadow into muscle, bone to a barrel of steel. For many years, you lie immobile. If the shadow is a thought, why can't you unthink it? On windy nights, the old trees inch toward the window.

If You Have Grown Unrecognizable to Yourself

It is your own doing. You were always setting off bombs in your own brain. Even as a child, light electric around your frizzy head. The only thing between your face and the shadow of your face in the creek was the meniscus, that rubbery boundary wrapping like lips around the stick you couldn't help but poke it with, a brief kiss before breaking.

Snow Angel

Angel of the bathtub. Angel of broken bottles in the creek. Angel of the last spoon of peanut butter in the jar. Angel of the rough bottom of the pool. Angel of running barefoot. Angel of being too shy to play Mary in the Christmas pageant, so much that you tried to blink it away, eyelids like two furious erasers. Angel of playing an angel. Angel of disappearing in a crowd of angels. Angel of the stuffed beagle tucked in the crook of your elbow. Angel of blood in the pool like a demon fleeing your body, gossamer-thin. Angel of mercurochrome. Angel of pinching open a snapdragon by the jaw. Angel of the roly-poly's conglobation. Angel of the tuck and roll. Angel of the snow globe where the snow falls only if you turn the world on its side and back again.

Therapy

Stand with your neck bare to the window. The principle of exposure is governed by how long the camera gazes at its subject. Visualize the shadow creeping behind you on the porch. The squeak of leather as he raises an arm. Exposure is saying *revolver* over and over until the word discharges its meaning. The exposure takes as long as it takes. Night passes. Clouds pass between you and the moon so you stand by turns in blindness and clarity. Stand until your heels root into the floorboards, until your limbs lengthen into vines. Your body flowers with honeysuckle, luring wild animals to the foyer. And you will wear an ammunition belt of hummingbirds around your hips, their shimmering, streamlined bodies. Nothing lives forever, not even planet Earth. But nothing lives by always dying. The exposure includes the bullet in your brain and the drifting continents of bone, remapping a world in which you will die or be reborn.

What the Bump in the Road Was

You are able to tell yourself it's not true. Think thoughts about other thoughts while behind you, in the dark, the mangled body drags itself into the trees. Roll to a slow and steady stop at the light. Carry your purse through the door. Sit in front of a deep red plate. The bump in the road was the rim of a black hole, the point where somethingness meets nothingness. The wheel jumping in your palms like a dead thing sprung to life. Somewhere, in the dark, the body lays its crushed head in the leaves. Swallow your bread. You haven't gone completely crazy.

Do You Have Less Energy than Usual

In the graveyard, one white stone charges toward the sky, a straight shot north from the brain buried below, a final prayer crystalized toward heaven. Squirrels find something else here, picking at the lumpy turf. It would be easier to relax if you were not imagining someone creeping behind you in the wind. The thing you like about squirrels is the white tips of their tail fur, how they seem lit up by some electricity. They know something you don't. You haven't even gotten out of the car. Your neck crooks over the open window frame waiting for the guillotine. The pine tree beckons with robed sleeves. The squirrels scramble into its arms. When you were little, you tried to hide your thoughts from God, but God sent an angel into your room to listen, and that made everything worse. You've come here to rest. The oldest coffins have collapsed their boards upon their inhabitants like the pleats of a wooden skirt. These are the kinds of things you think about: becoming dead, what the dead are wearing, what the animals claw from what was buried. A storm brews, and it's just like any other day. Someone somewhere blows a whistle. Someone will wake you up when it's time to go.

Beasts

After some time, you realized you had to get the beasts out of the house, so you dragged them by the horns to the farthest corner of the backyard. Look how they cower at the fence when the sprinkler spits at them in the summer. Don't explain to your friends when they gather, sipping dark soda on the deck. Everyone keeps something chained up. Eventually, in the sunshine, the beasts resign to slump over each other just so, snorting in their dreams, even purring. This is how you'll know you're turning a corner. Set out a kiddie pool for them to dip their hooves. Soon they'll lift their heads willingly for the collar. An enchanting jingle each time they haul themselves from slumber to stretch and resettle. See how they raise their hackles when the lawnmower rumbles near. You have trained them to fear the world outside their corner. You know a lot about fear. Sometimes, in the night, you float in your robe across the grass, set a hand on the warm, heaving mound. Their breathing sings the song of the tamed. A velvety puff at the end of each tail. From here, looking back at the glowing house, you can see everything through the windows.

A Fiery Ball of Fire

The house explodes while you sleep. You are standing next to the fireplace when the fireplace explodes. The microwave explodes in your face. The dryer explodes in your face. Gas leak in the oven. Gas leak in the underground line. Someone said you look like a porcelain doll. One of the other kids called you a ghost. Stand against a white wall, and no one can see you. While you sleep, the gas is a swarm of stars. You buy an escape ladder for every bedroom in the house. That one kid, years ago, didn't know what he was saying. Your own child runs into the snow in her polka dot pajamas, safe. Safe every time.

Transference

Lately, you don't feel the angel in your room. The dim shaft of white that attends the darkness is just a bathrobe limp at the closet door. On Sundays, you walk your daughter to Sunday School in her Mary Janes, your hands on her shoulders, steering her blindly toward God. Every Sunday, you wait in the hall while your child sings with the other children. When she runs off to join them, your hands collapse to your thighs, a short but dreadful plunge. At night, you lie in bed afraid the angel that has never left you has left you. The slender drape of your robe is a candlestick whose light is snuffed, whose wick smolders a dark ceiling over your body and the body of your husband who does not believe. In the evenings, a small voice across the hall. *This little light of mine.* The light is on in her room when you enter, sleepless. But she sleeps. Each night, she has kicked off her covers. Night by night, you are learning to leave her bared. She is not you. You believe in this new child come into the world despite you, entirely herself.

Syllabics

As if you could escape yourself, you take a walk to the lake where winter's ice recoils to shore, and across the surface, a wide blue eye awakens. A child's ball waits at the edge of the ice for the sun to tip it into the water. All winter, it has waited. You think, *no one has gone out to get it*. Ducks return, tottering in the wind. Ducks cluster at the rim of ice. Here, you count eight ducks: *no one has gone out to get it*. There, four ducks: *no one gets it*. You try not looking at ducks. The white flash of their under-tails, bobbing for weeds. Two ducks: *no one*. No thinking. A breeze on your neck. Shadows rippling toward you on the lake, dark stabby triangles. One two three: *triangles*. Try not counting these five ducks: *nobody gets it*. Nobody gets it. Go home. Spring is chronic. The mind is chronic.

Protection Spell Jar

Add to the jar the blinking. Counting to the number seven. Drawing a star. Counting to four. Gold flakes panned from the creek. The whisker of a stuffed dog. A salamander. Freckles. Star sticker pressed to the hem of a curtain. The ocean sand that scraped your cheek and the wave that turned your body over. The breath of air when you were no longer drowning. The first breath after choking and the sweet chocolate melted in your throat. Suspend disaster over the jar like a raindrop that pulls the fragile bloom down by its throat. The windshield wrapped around your body. Tapping in a pattern. Counting squares. The blazing heat of the star. The explosion.

It's Okay

If you're afraid of turbulence. Outside the window, whales levitate, heavy with rain. Remember that time the fire alarm went off at home? You went flying down the stairs and out the door while your family laughed, your mother flapping a towel at the oven door. But isn't that what you were supposed to do? Save yourself? You were afraid of other children playing down the street. How could you have known from their screams that someone hadn't sliced off a hand? And if some rowdy ghosts have wrapped their sheets around this airplane's wings and are now playing tug of war, that doesn't make you a baby. All of us are rocked by the whims of invisible forces. Remember that time your sister hid beneath the basement stairs, listening for your footfalls? And just before your foot landed, she shot her hand between the steps and screamed. You jumped and hit the wall. But you know what you had been afraid of? Hurting her. Listen, you should stop being afraid. Let this plane and every soul in it sink to the fiery core of the earth. You should have stomped on your sister's hand. That'll show them all. You should have sat in your room and burned.

Counting

You could have been counting the foxes tapping their claws across the street at night. You could have been counting diamonds hardening into ghostly fists that knock at the cellar door. The bulbous shells on the lakeshore among the many needle-sharp spiraled ones. Such a waste, hours lost to counting the windowpanes in this room. Even as, beyond the glass, eggs chipped open in the arm of the cottonwood tree, and the nest became an instrument of golden-mouthed horns. You're still here, counting in a pattern so the edges never touch, bouncing from translucent rectangle to translucent rectangle and back again in your mind, so no one else can see, as if this ritual would safeguard order in the world. But the baby bird is dragged off anyway by another bird. Your daughter's small hands fill with more needles than she can carry, and inside them, she hears the whispering oceans, all of them far away from you. Counting the fingers of your own hands again and again, a steady humming stupor like being carried off in a stream, bumping your head against the muddy banks as you go. You might have had a brilliant mind. But you were busy counting the four wheels beneath your bed. Often, come morning, you wake counting the lobbing paces of your heart. Have you done this all night in your sleep? There is a sort of grace in it, after all, counting yourself lucky to be alive.

4.

Trigger Point

Suppose you pull this drawer and release the knives, which have been waiting like spaceships rumbling with energy for the atmosphere to open. The filament fizzes in the lightbulb, a fish frenzied in a too-small bowl. The physical therapist says there are two types of muscles. One melts in his hands, lying down on command like a good dog. The other is concrete. The driveway in your neck rises steep from your first rib to the gate of your brain. It is time to forgive the tender meat of your heart its bundle of nerves. The loveliness of this cherry cabinet which holds its spices like a womb. How a child changes everything though she be but a fleck on the earth. How early in life you learned to wait for the bomb to go off before screaming, so as not to embarrass yourself. Imagine the release like coming upon a street on your daily walk, the nub of the dog's tail twitching its phantom wag, when suddenly the concrete bursts into hundreds of grey-winged moths lifting into the wind. The dog barks and barks. Forgive things their tense vibration. The knife is only looking to launch into the dark cadaver of space, far from this world. It only wishes, as you do, to dispatch from gravity, to feel weightless, reflecting this exquisite blue marble in its blade.

This Is How to Be Happy

When the blue day is puffed with clouds, you should be happy. Happiness is simple. Wear a rubber band around your wrist, so when you feel the impulse to drive the car head-on into another car, snap the band. When it's storming, you should also be happy. Heat lightning draws a serrated knife in the clouds. How many years did you cultivate this garden of negative thoughts like a prized rosebush? The roses in turn whispered suspicions with their velvety tongues. High in the canopy, the squirrel is pruning twigs for its nest. The dark language of foliage creeps at the garden gate. Sometimes, a cloud takes the perfect shape of a rabbit. And sometimes, lightning makes a squiggly line like a child's drawing, unrecognizable. It's okay if you're starting happiness from scratch.

Spoiler

You've already seen your future, and there was nothing in it but your own mind. Lying in a forest clearing, looking up, the sky was propped on a ring of trees like a crystal ball balanced on a fortune teller's fingertips. A cloud passed through like a brain, another like a wisp of thought. These voices in your head are all yours.

Choke

The universal sign for choking is a hand clamped to the throat like an animal fastening teeth to its prey. Death is almost always messy. Your mother's hands were swiftly at your shoulders, steering you from the love seat to the kitchen, bag of candies still crackling in your fist. Meanwhile, there is a great family narrative about your choking. Your sister ran to your father, who was mowing the lawn and the only one who knew what to do, but he ambled toward the house. Choking has many meanings. But your throat was glutted. Your throat was an underground burrow clogged with the hot frantic rabbit. You were the heat and the frenzy. Until some muscular force pushed you from behind. The countertop was a punch in the ribs, and the ball of chocolate shot into the sink like a small, wet heart. For twenty years you believed your mother had saved you. Surely it wasn't the angel that stood in your room at night, terrifying you to stillness. Not once did you guess you'd run into the kitchen on your own, thrown yourself against the sink as if you knew exactly how to save yourself. And even when you were dying, you knew to do it clean.

Heart Opener

If you push your heart toward the world, it will fly out of your chest toward the sky and be ruined forever. Yours is the heart that snarls in a tree. Not delicate like a kite ribboned in a blossoming branch but a lump wedged like a nest of squirrels, a bloody scene. There is too much at stake. Your daughter sleeps in a taut line, the latent velocity of a bird bounding on the wind with closed wings. You, leaning over to kiss her forehead still smelling of the day's sun, hollow your body around your heart like a net with an animal trapped inside. Across the room, in its dark tank, the tadpole sleeps with eyes open, stretching transparent hopeful legs, kissing the water in search of air to inflate the lungs blooming inside him. You will have to open your heart for the hard losses coming. Even the day will come that your daughter, on her pale lean legs, drops off the horizon of the farthest road, and nothing will stop her leaving you for the world. You will grow old and leave her in turn. Your arms already blotched by the sun like your mother's. You will lose everything. The frog turns a prairie green and eventually must be released to the pond. Clouds suspended there are swept away by the ripples of his arrival. Everything escapes your grasp. But for now, the blinds are snapped shut. Whatever she dreams, your daughter pulls her knees close. A lavender ruffle peeks from the beneath the quilt.

Spider

Alone on the basement stairs, you pinch the spider in a thick fold of paper towels, but you can still feel the awful pop of its body between your fingers. *Sorry*, you whisper to the kingdom of the dusty stairwell, *I'm sorry*, as if the delicate leggy ghost of the spider herself could hear. But not loud enough that your husband and daughter can hear. Returning to the kitchen, you are the hero bug-smasher, clasher of the cymbal that is the trash can clamping shut the dark grave of popsicle sticks and coffee grinds. No one would believe how fragile you are. But isn't that what you wanted? In labor with your only child, you masked your pain with water shushing from the faucet, husband exiled beyond the bathroom door. While your family sleeps, you check the yard for the serial killer who waits in the mud beneath the tree where the grass won't grow. Check that the moon still hangs above the roof. Are you the murderer or the murdered? Only the baby spiders in the wispy corner, too pale to see against the wall, know for sure.

Allow Your Strangers In

The serial killers. Men who trudge through the backyard at night with knives in their fists. Men who shuffle their boots through the leaves so loud you hear it through the blanket hooked over your ear. Shapeshifting men who transform into squirrels or deer the moment the moon of your forehead rises in the bedroom window. The angel bright as a lab coat dangling from a noose. The women who sit in their chairs with too many pillows and invite you to sit on their couches with too many pillows hard as taxidermied animals pressing their muzzles at your hip. Women who jot on their clipboards. Helicopters that thump the roof of your house at night, throwing their lights at the trees in hopes of illuminating men escaped from the prison. Invite them into your home to gather by the fire. Invite even the stranger you met on the trail when you were too young to be riding in the woods alone. His dazed and bloodied face, the way he looked straight into your eyes but didn't seem to see you. How you knew you could pretend to be an apparition. How you left him stumbling in his orange tennis shoes, his bicycle jackknifed in the weeds, wheel still spinning with a hiss. How you just kept pumping your feet.

Of Feather

If you stare into the dark hard enough, something glitters. You lie steady, quilt pressed to your throat, hemmed in by spirits. Your husband passes through the dark to the dresser unbothered, swinging his long arms. Now whipping out the flag of his pajama pants. One leg at a time, bright skin erased by fabric. Is this what it will be like when he dies? The two of you lie on your backs like children shoulder to shoulder in an overgrown field. The forest blustery with ghosts. What if he's right? The ceiling clamps shut over your body. What if there will be nothing? He sleeps. You wake. The angel leaning over you now is a sizzle of electricity. But you don't hear a thing. Over time, you've learned to pack tissues in your ears, listen only to the static crackling in your own head. An angel is a wisp of feather crossing the back of your mind. Proof of nothing. If a feather hisses to the floor, you don't hear it. You will not hear the door unfastening in the night.

Vanishing Act

You have lost something. In the way that, as a child, you once lost a road. You ran through the tunnel in the earth beneath the asphalt but couldn't understand how it was possible to come out the other side into sunlight. Through the trees, you could hear cars. A sea monster eating children from a crowd of children. The hedge opened its mouth, and you crawled inside and were swallowed. These days, it seems as if your whole world fits inside this green bowl. The daily folding of bread around a dull blade. The sagging bruise on a peach. Is there a name for when floaters play tricks in your eyes, filling the air with the sinking detritus of sea creatures? Those childhood summers when tadpoles turned in the bucket like compass needles searching for north. That final morning you stepped outside to find the emptied pool still sloshing. The vanishing act was always quicker than you expected. Once, the cat pressed a mouse beneath her paws before you could stop her. A ripple steered through the grass, evidence of its quick and fantastic escape.

The Red Suitcase

You had a doll in a red suitcase. Your mother stands at the window where the trees glow faintly in the light that reaches them from the kitchen. Her reflection haunts the forest wearing her green robe. *My memory's going*, she says. Beneath the basement stairs, a spider waits, laying out a silver wig for your hair. The garage is a chilled lake seeping through your slippers. Doorknobs turn. Nights, the suitcase swings open. Rising from her burial dresses, a flash of the doll's bony cheek. A chill climbs your leg. You get up. Shelves in the closet. Shelves in the study. Your arms turn feathery with dust. Somewhere her unbending feet. The laces of her shoes like vines growing wild in some forgotten garden. Close your eyes, she comes to you. She floats from the shelf, dragging her hair behind her. The ghost of your mother stares directly into your mother's eyes. The suitcase is a hard red bird winging past.

Trash Angel

This cigarette fallen on the gas station tarmac in its long white robe. This half-eaten fruit in the trash bin turning to rot. These napkins swept in an updraft like hands lifted to prayer. There's nothing to be afraid of. You do not fear the pine tree covered in snow, despite its ghostly dress. The forest is chainsawed at the ankles. Have mercy. Angels are moved by the winds, just as you are. Just as the scarf blows over your eyes the moment your child stumbles. You can sometimes protect her, sometimes not. The rats in the sewer receive their blessings quickly, before the paper wings floating past disintegrate in the current. You could, perhaps, be the angel. Except when winter comes, you are the one driving the truck home with the angel strapped to the roof. A jingle on the radio. You will bind its body in holiday lights. Feed it water in a bowl for a little while, for as long as it keeps its sweetness, until you have no use for it anymore.

Trigger Warning

How fat the nest is getting year after year. The extra tuft of twigs that dangled in the wind for weeks before finally dropping to the deck. You swept it away. Loving anything. Loving this world. Your mother hoisting her bird feeders on a pulley in the forest where you were young. Her house wreathed in flowers like a horse with the winning garland hooped around its neck. Your own dry garden, a shy blush of pink by the stairs. The neighbors who turned off their nature camera after all the eggs were taken from the nest one by one. Ghosts you called for reassurance but never answered. Those you know by name and those you don't. The bird your sister rehabilitated in the bathroom until the day it flapped through the open window into the trees and did not return. The squirrel you've watched tending her babies now splayed flat on the porch. You scare her away just to know she's alive. The bird bath is a shimmering coin of riches. The time you thought you had so much of.

Uncertainty

You will only be cured of the uncertainty about your own death after you die, so what good does it do? Tonight, the rabbits run in the wet grass, white tails bobbing like lifeboats on turbulent seas. You are invited to sit with uncertainty. Sit in this porch chair in need of paint by the prickly weeds fattening in the garden. Everywhere, the great unknown is murmuring. Today, walking barefoot through the yard, you found tufts of fur, a curl of entrails from which a single red berry had tumbled. You tried opening a door for the ghosts to shuttle through, but they held tight to the shadows. You always blocked your ears, anyway, humming like the child you still are against the truth you refuse to hear. You cannot go on flinching at each small thing. See how the rabbits ride the current, trimming the sails of their ears to the wind. Surely the dead had a good last meal. Surely that berry broke a bright tang against her teeth.

MRI Machine

Strapped inside this bright rocket, you are a spirit ready to be launched toward the light. A technician watches through the window. A wire goes into your ear through which her voice arrives. The robotic dial clocks the years you've lived in pain. Lie still. You've been good. You've persevered. The hum and snap of magnets turns a mechanical halo around your brain. Music blooms from the end of the wire. A child sings a song that will play in your head for months, tangled in the nub of disquiet deep inside your neck. Nothing changes. You will tense your shoulders just as always, until the muscles harden into birds whose feet are stitched into the fascia of your body and cannot fly away. They will sing the song of worry that accompanies you to your grave. The real one. The one you do not come out of as you do today, sliding back into the fluorescence of the examination room, where a hand now clasps you by the wrist to help you up.

A Great Many Things

In the bath, a galaxy of bubbles collapses in a weightless, glittering mound, marking the end of another day in which you are not dead. Your body and all its invisible particles stitched tightly together. Sink deeper into this warm white cradle, weary from the rattling of your own mind. At dusk, walking through the field, you picked a feather from the grass and ran its shimmering vane between your knuckles. You wanted to see how it was held together by peeling apart its hooks and barbs. There was a hush about it, the swish of hands releasing their grasp. You saw how easily the delicate design of the world can be undone. But for now, you are safe in this watery embrace. Each alternate universe bursts around you one by one, releasing a held breath. A great many things will happen to you, but none of the things you are afraid of. It was the wind in your hair. The red-winged birds embroidering the blue sky. That has been your life.

Shells

Each shell is a spiral staircase you have climbed. A hermit crab you glued a hook to and leashed with yarn to walk in the yard like an intelligent, trainable pet. You could connect two shells with string and play telephone with the opposite shore or your childhood self. What else could occupy these tiny cones but a tongue, a long slip of meat? Shells pointy enough you could stab someone, as long as you stood close and didn't wish to do real harm. The fact is, today you are happy. Your daughter is near in her winter puffer but feet bare in the lake. She kneels to stroke the green algae that coats a rock like the pelt of a drowned animal. You wouldn't know if the telephone was working because your child self is too shy to speak. Without its tongue, what remains of the shell is the resonator. The wind passing through makes a vibrating engine of music. Your daughter climbs the lifeguard tower. The song in your hands is quiet, but today you can hear the tiniest of voices, the miniature piccolo trumpet, smaller than a fingernail, high-pitched, hysterical, and wild.

ACKNOWLEDGMENTS

Grateful acknowledgment is made to the editors and readers of the following journals and anthologies in which these poems first appeared, some in earlier versions or with different titles:

Alaska Quarterly Review: "The Red Suitcase"
Bennington Review: "Quality of Life"
Birdcoat Quarterly: "Counting," "Trigger Point"
CALYX Journal: "You Believe"
Columbia: A Journal of Literature and Art: "You with the Getting Shot," 2014 Poetry Contest winner, reprinted in *New Poetry from the Midwest 2017* (anthology)
DIALOGIST: "Stipulations"
Diode: "In the Forest," "It Starts," "The Face Has Seven Holes," "The Music of Language Is Clamping Down Hard," "You Get a Thought in Your Head"
Electric Literature's *The Commuter:* "Diagnosis," "Seven Darknesses," "Therapy"
elsewhere: "Choke," "Spoiler"
Image: "Trash Angel"
Jubilat: "A Fiery Ball of Fire"
Lake Effect: "Intrusive," "Ruminate"
Mid-American Review: "Open Window"
Milk Journal: "Like This"
Moon City Review: "Trigger Warning"
Nimrod International Journal: "Shells"
Pithead Chapel: "Field Guide to the Proper Identification of Roadside Debris"
Poetry Northwest: "Angel Number Seven," "Conkers"
Porter House Review: "Scar"
Radar Poetry: "Touched"
Rogue Agent: "MRI Machine"
Salamander: "The Phantom"

Sepia Journal: "Vanishing Act"

Smartish Pace: "None of This Happened," "Spider"

South Dakota Review: "Balaclava," "Simultaneity," "What the Bump in the Road Was"

Sugar House Review: "House Inside the House"

Superstition Review: "If You Have Grown Unrecognizable to Yourself," "Protection Spell Jar," "This Is All True"

SWWIM Every Day: "Dark Matter"

The Believer: "The Angel"

The Eloquent Poem: 128 Contemporary Poems and Their Making, 2019 (anthology): "Smoke When You Can't See What's on Fire"

The Indianapolis Review: "This Is How to Be Happy"

The Journal: "It's Okay"

The Los Angeles Review: "Exploding Head Syndrome," "Heart Opener"

The Missouri Review: "Allow Your Strangers In," "Blood Moon," "Snow Angel," "Recording Angel," "Uncertainty"

The Night Heron Barks: "Corpse Meditation"

The Shore: "Syllabics"

The Texas Review: "A Great Many Things," "Do You Have Less Energy than Usual," "Of Feather"

Tinderbox Poetry Journal: "Transference"

Unsplendid: "Intersection"

With deep gratitude to the fellow poets and friends who read and critiqued these poems and who helped me believe I could write this book: Jesse Lee Kercheval, Nick Lantz, J.L. Conrad, Nina Clements, Jennifer Fandel, Sarah Kain Gutowski, Jenny Sadre-Orafai, Nancy Reddy, Rebecca Dunham, Rita Mae Reese, Angela Voras-Hills, Erin Ruzicka Trondson, Jason Gray, and many others not named here. Thank you to Eugenia Leigh for the generous blurb and for getting it. And thank you to the artist Sandra Boskamp for use of her stunning oil painting on the cover. And always, to my family.

Thank you to Gabriel Fried and Persea Books for their continued support and for their belief in my work.